Muffin Cookbook

Delicious Muffin Recipes for Overall Health

BY

Stephanie Sharp

License Notes

Table of Contents

Introduction

Nothing is better than eating good food with your family and spending some quality time with them at the breakfast table.

With this book, you can get plenty of ideas about different kinds of muffins that you can prepare every day for your loved ones and they would never get bored of them.

Feel free to choose from plenty of famous muffin recipes such as Blueberry Muffins, Eggless Vanilla Muffins, Spice Pumpkin Muffins, Banana Nut Muffins, Strawberry Oatmeal Muffins, Maple-Sweetened Banana Muffins, Sugar-Crusted Raspberry Muffins, Rhubarb Breakfast Muffins, Cinnamon Sugar Pumpkin Muffins, Whole Wheat Apple

Cinnamon Muffins, Bran Muffins, Carrot Currant Muffins, Mini Blueberry Muffins with Streusel, and so on.

Just tune the pages and amaze your family with your cooking skills.

Recipes

Best Ever Muffins

Prep Time: 10 minutes

Cooking Time: 30 minutes

Servings: 12 persons

For raisin/dates muffins, feel free to add 1 cup of finely chopped raisins/dates into the prepared batter. You can even add ½ cup of chocolate chips and can increase the amount of vanilla extract.

Ingredients

- 1 organic egg, large-sized
- 1 cup milk
- 2 cups of all-purpose flour
- ¾ cup white sugar
- 3 teaspoons baking powder
- ¼ cup vegetable oil
- ½ teaspoon salt

Directions

Preheat your oven to 400 F in advance.

Stir the flour with baking powder, sugar and salt in a large-sized mixing bowl until mixed well. Make a well in middle. Next, beat the egg using a fork in a 2-cup measuring cup or small-sized mixing bowl. Stir in oil and milk. Immediately pour into the formed well in flour mixture. Quickly mix the ingredients using a fork till moistened, ensure that you don't beat the ingredients. Fill paper lined muffin pan cups with the prepared batter.

Bake in the preheated oven until turn golden brown, for 20 to 25 minutes.

Serve immediately and enjoy.

Nutritional Value: kcal: 160, Fat: 4.6 g, Fiber: 0.4 g, Protein: 3.1 g

Blueberry Muffins

Prep Time: 10 minutes

Cooking Time: 40 minutes

Servings: 12 persons

Just try making this recipe when fresh blueberries are in season. I am sure that these delicious muffins would disappear in minutes and everyone would love the taste. You can even use full-fat plain yogurt recipe in this recipe. Absolutely delicious and healthy!

Ingredients

- 1 cup plain yogurt, low fat
- 1 to 1 ½ cups blueberries, fresh or frozen
- ½ cup granulated white sugar
- 1 lightly beaten egg, large
- ½ teaspoon baking soda
- 1 teaspoon pure vanilla extract
- 2 cups all-purpose flour
- 1/3 cup safflower, canola, vegetable, or corn oil
- 1 ¼ teaspoons baking powder
- ¼ teaspoon salt

Directions

Line a standard-sized muffin tin (with 12 muffin cups) with paper liners or coat it lightly with the butter.

Next, position a rack in middle of your oven and then, preheat your oven to 375 F in advance.

Whisk the beaten egg with yogurt, vanilla extract, and oil in a large-sized mixing bowl until mixed well.

Whisk the flour with baking soda, sugar, baking powder & salt in a separate large-sized mixing bowl until mixed well. Gently stir in the fresh blueberries. Fold the wet ingredients into dry ingredients using a rubber spatula, give the ingredients a good stir until the ingredients are moistened and combined well.

Fill the lined muffin cups evenly with the prepared batter, using an ice cream scoop or two spoons. Place in the preheated oven & bake until a toothpick comes out clean, for 17 to 20 minutes. Transfer to a wire rack & let cool for 10 minutes then, remove from the pan

Nutritional Value: kcal: 189, Fat: 6.2 g, Fiber: 1 g, Protein: 3.4 g

Cinnamon Muffins

Prep Time: 10 minutes

Cooking Time: 20 minutes

Servings: 16 persons

To increase the moistness and richness, feel free to replace the milk with buttermilk. You can even fill the muffins with jam, preferably in the middle.

Ingredients

- 2 cups all-purpose flour
- 1 tablespoon cinnamon
- 4 teaspoons baking powder
- 1 cup sugar
- 2 organic eggs, large-sized
- 1 cup milk
- 2 tablespoons sugar
- ½ cup vegetable oil
- 1 teaspoon cinnamon
- ½ teaspoon salt

Directions

Grease a muffin tin with 16 muffins cups and then, preheat your oven to 375 F in advance.

Combine flour with cinnamon, baking powder, sugar & salt in a large-sized mixing bowl until mixed well.

Beat the milk with eggs, and vegetable oil in a separate bowl. Make a well in middle of dry ingredients and then, add in the mixture of wet ingredients, give the ingredients a good stir until just combined, ensure you don't over mix the ingredients.

Next, fill the prepared muffin cups evenly with the prepared mixture.

Combine the sugar with cinnamon in a small-sized mixing bowl. Sprinkle the cups with the prepared cinnamon sugar mixture.

Bake in the preheated oven for 13 to 15 minutes, until a toothpick comes out clean.

Nutritional Value: kcal: 184, Fat: 6 g, Fiber: 2 g, Protein: 2 g

Eggless Vanilla Muffins

Prep Time: 10 minutes

Cooking Time: 55 minutes

Servings: 15 persons

For flavoring, you can use chocolate chips in this recipe. For added nutrition, I often serve this recipe with a glass full of almond milk.

Ingredients

- 2 cups flour
- ½ cup butter
- 2 teaspoons vinegar
- 1 cup milk
- 2 teaspoons vanilla
- ½ cup sugar, powdered
- 2 teaspoons baking powder

Directions

Combine the flour with butter, sugar and baking powder in a large-sized mixing bowl until mixed well.

Add milk followed by vinegar, and vanilla, continue to mix the ingredients. Beat the batter until completely smooth. Fill approximately 20 muffin moulds with the prepared batter.

Bake in the preheated oven until a toothpick comes out clean, for 20 to 25 minutes.

Serve warm and enjoy.

Nutritional Value: kcal: 196, Fat: 6 g, Fiber: 5 g, Protein: 6 g

Delicious Homemade Muffins

Prep Time: 10 minutes

Cooking Time: 20 minutes

Servings: 8 persons

These delicious muffins taste amazing with savory add-ins such as garlic and cheddar. You can even add pecan pieces and apple-flavored cranberries. Rather than using the regular sugar, you can use Splenda instead.

Ingredients

- ¼ cup vegetable oil
- 1 ½ cups flour all-purpose
- ½ cup milk, any of your favorite
- 1 beaten egg, large-sized
- 2 teaspoons baking powder
- ½ cup sugar
- 1 teaspoon vanilla extract
- ½ teaspoon salt

Directions

Grease a muffin pan well or line it with muffin papers then, preheat your oven to 400 F in advance.

Combine egg with vegetable oil and milk.

Next, combine the flour with baking powder, sugar & salt in a separate medium-sized mixing bowl, whisk until combined well. Once done, mix both the ingredients well & blend until combined well.

Fill each muffin paper approximately 2/3 full with the prepared batter & bake in the preheated oven until a toothpick comes out clean, for 16 to 20 minutes. Store in a large container or an airtight bag.

Nutritional Value: kcal: 202, Fat: 6 g, Fiber: 2 g, Protein: 2 g

Toasted Coconut Pear Muffins

Prep Time: 40 minutes

Cooking Time: 20 minutes

Servings: 18 persons

Absolutely delicious and a savior! You can sub the vanilla bean paste with vanilla extract. If you don't have milk or yogurt, then you can use coconut milk instead.

Ingredients

- 2 cups pears, diced into ½" pieces
- ¼ teaspoon ground cardamom
- 2 cups flour
- 1 teaspoon baking soda
- 2 organic eggs, large-sized
- 1 ¼ teaspoons baking powder
- ½ cup unsweetened, plain Greek yogurt
- 2 teaspoons vanilla extract
- ½ cup brown sugar
- 1 cup milk
- ½ cup sugar
- 1 ¼ cups shredded sweetened coconut, toasted, keep ½ cup aside for topping
- ½ teaspoon salt

For Topping

- 1 teaspoon vanilla bean paste
- ½ cup sugar, powdered
- 2 tablespoons milk
- ½ cup coconut toasted, shredded

Directions

Spray muffin tins with non-stick cooking spray or line with papers and then, preheat your oven to 350 F in advance.

Whisk flour with baking soda, baking powder, and ground cardamom in a large-sized mixing bowl until mixed well, set the mix aside

Next, combine the eggs with white sugar, brown sugar and salt using an electric mixer (attached with a paddle attachment) in a large bowl. Beat the ingredients for a minute or two and then, add vanilla, yogurt & milk, continue to mix the ingredients until combined well.

Slowly add the dry ingredients into the wet ingredients and continue to mix the ingredients until combined well.

Using hands, fold in the toasted coconut and diced pears, filling the muffin tin approximately ¾ full.

Bake in the preheated oven until a toothpick comes out clean, for 12 to 15 minutes. Remove the muffins from tin & let them completely cool on a wire rack then, add the topping.

For Topping

Combine the vanilla paste with powdered sugar. Add milk and continue to mix until thin enough to drizzle. Once done, drizzle on top of each muffin & top with the toasted coconut.

Store the muffins in a covered container for up to two days in the refrigerator.

Nutritional Value: kcal: 161, Fat: 3 g, Fiber: 1 g, Protein: 2 g

Cherry Almond Muffins with Almond Flour

Prep Time: 20 minutes

Cooking Time: 30 minutes

Servings: 14 persons

These muffins are one of the best muffins that I have ever tasted. You can even add your favorite nuts to this recipe. Absolutely healthy & delicious!

Ingredients

- 3 cups blanched almond flour
- 2 teaspoons baking powder
- ½ cup sliced almonds plus extra for garnish
- 2 lightly beaten eggs, large-sized
- ½ cup sour cream
- ½ cup sugar
- 1 teaspoon vanilla extract
- 8 oz roughly chopped cherries
- ½ teaspoon salt

Directions

Grease each cup of the muffin tin with cooking oil or line the cups with liners and then, preheat your oven to 350 F.

Combine almond flour with baking powder, sugar, and salt, whisk the ingredients well.

Next, whisk sour cream with eggs, and vanilla extract in a separate bowl and then, fold the mix into the dry ingredients, give the ingredients a good stir until just combined.

Gently fold in the sliced nuts and cherries.

Fill each muffin cup approximately ¾ full with the prepared batter and then, garnish with sliced almonds.

Bake in the preheated oven for 20 to 25 minutes, until a toothpick comes out clean.

Let completely cool in the pan before serving. Serve and enjoy.

Nutritional Value: kcal: 217, Fat: 14 g, Fiber: 2.4 g, Protein: 6.2 g

Spice Pumpkin Muffins

Prep Time: 20 minutes

Cooking Time: 20 minutes

Servings: 16 persons

These soft & tender muffins are absolutely delicious. If you a fan of streusel, then you can top your muffins with them as well!

Ingredients

- 1½ cups all-purpose flour
- 1 teaspoon baking soda
- ½ cup whole wheat flour
- 1 teaspoon baking powder
- 2 teaspoon cinnamon
- ½ teaspoon ground cloves
- ½ teaspoon ground nutmeg
- 1 cup pumpkin puree, canned
- ½ cup white sugar
- 4 oz cream cheese, at room temperature
- ½ cup brown sugar
- 2 organic eggs, large-sized
- ½ cup nut milk or non-fat milk
- 2 teaspoons vanilla extract
- ½ teaspoon salt

For Garnish:

- 1/8 cup sugar, powdered

Directions

Preheat your oven to 350 F in advance. Lightly grease the muffin pan or line it with cupcake liners.

Add cream cheese with brown sugar, and white sugar using an electric mixer in a large-sized mixing bowl. Continue to mix the ingredients for 2 to 3 minutes, until light & fluffy, on medium-high.

Slowly add the eggs & continue to beat the ingredients after each addition. Once done, add the pumpkin, milk, and vanilla extract. Continue to mix the ingredients for a minute or two more, until blended well.

Next, combine the flours with nutmeg, cinnamon, baking soda, baking powder, cloves, and salt in a separate medium-sized mixing bowl. Whisk the ingredients until combined well.

Slowly blend the dry ingredients into pumpkin mixture using the mixer, on low speed.

Fill the prepared muffin cups approximately ¾ full with the prepared mixture & bake in the preheated oven till a toothpick comes out clean, for 17 to 20 minutes, turning once during the baking time.

Remove the baked muffins to a cooling rack to cool.

Once done, dust with the powdered sugar. Serve and enjoy.

Nutritional Value: kcal: 150, Fat: 2 g, Fiber: 1 g, Protein: 2 g

Lemon Pistachio Muffins

Prep Time: 20 minutes

Cooking Time: 20 minutes

Servings: 14 persons

Absolutely delicious and healthy! These muffins can be frozen for a couple of days too, just reheat the same when serving.

Ingredients

- 1 organic egg, large
- 1 ¼ teaspoons baking powder
- 2 cups all-purpose flour
- 1 teaspoon baking soda
- 1 ¼ cups whole milk
- Zest & juice of 1 lemon, fresh
- ½ cup coarsely ground pistachios
- 1 teaspoon lemon extract
- ¾ cup sugar
- 1 tablespoon flour
- ½ teaspoon salt

For Glaze:

- ½ teaspoon lemon extract
- 1 cup sugar, powdered
- ¼ cup whole milk

Directions

Lightly grease 2 muffin tins (with 12 cups) with butter, oil, or even non-stick cooking spray and then, preheat your oven to 350 F.

For Muffins:

Combine the juice from one lemon with milk, set the mixture aside for a couple of minutes.

Combine the flour with baking soda, baking powder, and salt in a large-sized mixing bowl, whisk the ingredients until mixed well, set aside.

Next, combine sugar with egg & the prepared lemon juice-milk mixture using an electric stand mixer in a large bowl. Blend well and then, add in the lemon extract and lemon zest, continue to blend the ingredients until completely smooth.

Slowly add the dry ingredients into the wet ingredients.

Combine the ground pistachios with a tablespoon of the flour. Fold this mixture into the prepared batter.

Bake in the preheated oven until a toothpick comes out clean, for 12 to 15 minutes. Once done, remove the muffins carefully from the muffin pan & let cool on a wire rack for a couple of minutes.

For Glaze

Combine all of the glaze ingredients together in a medium-sized mixing bowl. Feel free to add more of powdered sugar or milk, if required until you get maple syrup like consistency.

Dip a large fork in the prepared glaze and lightly shake on top of cooled muffins.

Nutritional Value: kcal: 179, Fat: 2 g, Fiber: 1 g, Protein: 3 g

Chocolate Muffins

Prep Time: 10 minutes

Cooking Time: 40 minutes

Servings: 15 persons

For chocolaty taste, you can spread a few chocolate scraps on top.

Ingredients

- 100 g melted butter
- 5 tablespoons chocolate topping, any of your favorite
- 180 ml milk, preferably full-cream
- 250 g bake mix, eggless

Directions

Preheat your oven to 350 F in advance.

Combine the bake mix with milk and butter in a large-sized mixing bowl until the batter is completely smooth.

Lightly coat the muffin moulds and then, line them with the muffin liners. Fill each with approximately ¾ of the prepared batter.

Bake in the preheated oven until a toothpick comes out clean, for 30 minutes.

Remove the muffins from muffin moulds & arrange them on a large-sized serving plate. Top each muffin with the dessert topping chocolate, serve immediately & enjoy.

Nutritional Value: kcal: 304, Fat: 1.1 g, Fiber: 2.1 g, Protein: 3 g

Banana Muffins

Prep Time: 20 minutes

Cooking Time: 30 minutes

Servings: 10 persons

If you are looking for an eggless and vegan version of the muffins, then you must go for this recipe. Rather than using the oil, feel free to use melted butter.

Ingredients

Wet Ingredients:

- 5 medium bananas or 3 large bananas
- Juice of one lemon or lime, fresh
- ¼ cup organic cane sugar, unrefined
- 1 teaspoon vanilla powder or vanilla extract
- ½ cup oil

Dry Ingredients:

- ½ teaspoon baking soda
- 1 ½ cups whole wheat flour
- 1 teaspoon baking powder
- A pinch of salt

Directions

Line a muffin tray with muffin liners and then, preheat your oven to 350 F in advance.

For Batter:

Mash the chopped bananas with sugar in a large-sized mixing bowl using a masher or a fork, don't worry, if small chunks of bananas remain.

Next, whisk in the oil until evenly mixed.

Add vanilla powder or extract, give the ingredients a good stir and then, add 1 tablespoon of lemon or lime juice. Mix well & set aside, until required.

Sieve 1 ½ cups of whole wheat flour with 1 teaspoon baking powder, ½ teaspoon baking soda and a pinch of salt in the bowl with wet ingredients.

Gently fold the dry ingredients with wet ingredients using a spatula, with light hands. Don't over mix the folding.

For Baking:

Fill the liners approximately ¾ full with the prepared batter.

Place the muffin tray in middle rack & bake until a toothpick comes out dry or with few crumb particles, for 30 to 35 minutes.

Serve as dessert or sweet snack.

Nutritional Value: kcal: 203, Fat: 7 g, Fiber: 2 g, Protein: 1 g

Banana Nut Muffins

Prep Time: 10 minutes

Cooking Time: 30 minutes

Servings: 12 persons

Enjoy these delicious muffins as a breakfast recipe. Feel free to use self-rising flour and brown sugar in this recipe. I often serve mine with a glass full of coconut/almond milk.

Ingredients

- 1 cup pecans or walnuts, chopped (raw or toasted)
- 2 to 3 ripe bananas, mashed thoroughly (approximately 1 ¼ cups)
- 1 teaspoon vanilla extract
- 1/3 cup butter, melted
- 1 beaten egg, large-sized
- ¾ cup sugar
- 1 tablespoon strong espresso or brewed coffee
- 1 ½ cups flour
- 1 teaspoon baking soda
- A pinch of salt

Directions

Line a muffin pan with paper liners and then, preheat your oven to 350 F in advance.

Next, in a large-sized mixing bowl, thoroughly mash the bananas and then, stir in the melted butter followed by egg, sugar, vanilla extract and coffee.

Whisk the flour with baking soda & salt.

Slowly add the flour mixture into the banana mixture, give the ingredients a good stir after each addition until just incorporated.

Fold in the chopped pecans or walnuts.

Fill the prepared muffin tin approximately ¾ full with the prepared mixture. Bake in the preheated oven until a toothpick comes out clean, for 17 to 20 minutes. Once done, let them cool on a rack. Serve immediately and enjoy.

Nutritional Value: kcal: 121, Fat: 0.2 g, Fiber: 1.2 g, Protein: 4.6 g

Zucchini Muffins

Prep Time: 20 minutes

Cooking Time: 30 minutes

Servings: 12 persons

Rather than using the butter, feel free to use margarine or vegetable oil for this recipe. You can also use dates instead of raisins and enjoy.

Ingredients

- 2 organic eggs, large-sized
- ½ teaspoon nutmeg
- 1 cup walnuts
- 2 teaspoons vanilla extract
- 1 teaspoon baking soda
- ¾ cup unsalted butter, melted
- 1 1/3 cups sugar
- 2 ¾ cups all-purpose flour
- 3 cups fresh zucchini, packed, grated
- 1 teaspoon ground ginger
- 2 teaspoons cinnamon
- 1 teaspoon baking powder
- 1 cup dried cranberries or raisins
- ¼ teaspoon salt

Directions

Preheat your oven to 350 F in advance.

Beat the eggs in a large-sized mixing bowl. Mix in the vanilla extract and sugar and then, stir in the melted butter and grated zucchini.

Next, combine the flour with nutmeg, cinnamon, baking powder, baking soda, ground ginger, and salt in a separate medium-sized bowl.

Stir the mixture of dry ingredients into the prepared zucchini mixture. Ensure that you don't over mix the ingredients and then, stir in the walnuts, cranberries or raisins.

Coat your muffin pan or each muffin cup with a bit of vegetable oil or butter and then, fill each with approximately ¾ full of the prepared batter.

Bake in the preheated oven for 20 to 30 minutes, until muffins turn golden brown and a toothpick comes out clean.

Set on the wire rack for 5 minutes to cool down. Remove the muffins carefully from the tin & let cool for 10 more minutes.

Nutritional Value: kcal: 314, Fat: 16 g, Fiber: 2.2 g, Protein: 4.8 g

Strawberry Oatmeal Muffins

Prep Time: 20 minutes

Cooking Time: 30 minutes

Servings: 12 persons

Feel free to add a handful of fresh blueberries or cranberries to this recipe, if desired. You can even use peach mango yogurt as well.

Ingredients

- ½ pound strawberries
- 1 cup non-fat plain Greek yogurt
- ½ teaspoon cinnamon
- 2 organic eggs, large-sized
- 1 ¼ cups old fashioned oats
- 2 teaspoons granulated white sugar
- ½ cup melted butter, unsalted
- ¼ teaspoon salt
- 1 teaspoon balsamic vinegar
- ½ cup packed brown sugar
- 1 teaspoon vanilla extract
- ½ teaspoon baking soda
- 1 cup all purpose flour
- ¼ teaspoon finely ground black pepper
- 1 tablespoon baking powder

Directions

Combine the oats with yogurt in a large-sized mixing bowl.

Rinse & core the fresh strawberries and then, chop them roughly. Place them in a small-sized mixing bowl.

Sprinkle with balsamic vinegar and white sugar, give the ingredients a gentle stir and ensure that the strawberries are nicely coated with the vinegar and sugar.

Position a rack in the center position of your oven and then, preheat the oven to 400 F.

Coat a muffin tin with 12-well lightly with butter.

Whisk the flour with baking soda, baking powder, cinnamon, black pepper and salt in a medium-sized mixing bowl

Add eggs followed by brown sugar, melted butter & vanilla extract to the yogurt-oatmeal mixture, give it a good stir until just incorporated.

Next, stir the prepared flour mixture into the oatmeal mixture using a large wooden spoon.

Gently fold in the roughly chopped strawberries (including the sugary vinegary liquid).

Fill the prepared tin wells approximately ¾ full with the prepared batter.

Bake in the preheated oven for 17 to 20 minutes, until a toothpick comes out clean.

Remove from the oven and let cool in the muffin tin for a few minutes. Carefully remove the muffins from the tin and serve.

Nutritional Value: kcal: 187, Fat: 8.5 g, Fiber: 1.4 g, Protein: 4.2 g

Chocolate Cranberry Zucchini Muffins

Prep Time: 20 minutes

Cooking Time: 30 minutes

Servings: 12 persons

Absolutely delicious, nutritious, refreshing, and healthy! I added green pistachios but you can use cashews and/or almonds in this recipe.

Ingredients

- 1 ½ teaspoons baking powder
- 1 cup all-purpose flour
- 1/3 cup Dutch process cocoa powder, unsweetened
- 1 cup almond flour
- ½ teaspoon baking soda
- 1 teaspoon ground cinnamon
- 1/3 cup honey
- 2 organic eggs, large-sized
- ¼ cup buttermilk
- 1 cup whole cranberries, fresh or frozen
- 3 cups zucchini, grated
- 1 teaspoon vanilla extract
- 3 tablespoons green pistachios, chopped
- ¼ cup olive oil
- 2 tablespoons turbinado sugar
- ½ teaspoon salt

Directions

Place a rack in middle of your oven and then, preheat your oven to 400 F in advance.

Generously coat the cups & rims of a standard-sized muffin tin (12-cups) with butter.

Next, whisk the almond flour with all-purpose flour, baking soda, baking powder, cocoa powder, cinnamon & salt in a large-sized mixing bowl until mixed well.

Make a well in middle of your bowl & break the eggs into it. Once done, immediately add in the buttermilk, honey, vanilla, and oil. Thoroughly mix the ingredients using a fork, give the ingredients a good stir until the flour is incorporated well.

Stir in the cranberries and zucchini.

Fill each coated muffin cup approximately 1/3 cup full with the prepared batter using an ice cream scoop.

Sprinkle with the pistachios and turbinado sugar, set the tin carefully on a large-sized baking sheet.

Bake in the preheated oven until a toothpick comes out with few crumbs, for 23 to 25 minutes.

Once done, place the tin with muffins on a rack and let cool for a couple of minutes.

Remove the muffins carefully from the pan & let completely cool on the rack.

Nutritional Value: kcal: 212, Fat: 10 g, Fiber: 2.7 g, Protein: 4.9 g

Eggless Blueberry Muffins

Prep Time: 20 minutes

Cooking Time: 30 minutes

Servings: 12 persons

The granulated sugar is optional in this recipe. If you don't want to use it, then you can skip using it. The best part about these muffins is that you can cover and store them at room temperature for 3 to 4 days.

Directions

Lightly coat the cups of your muffin tin (12 cups) with non-stick cooking spray or butter and then, preheat your oven to 325 F in advance.

Next, beat the maple syrup with coconut oil in a large-sized mixing bowl using a whisk. Slowly add the organic eggs & continue to beat the ingredients for a minute more. Mix in the milk and mashed bananas, followed by vanilla extract, baking soda, cinnamon and salt.

Add the oats and flour to the bowl & continue to mix the ingredients until just combined using a large spoon.

Evenly divide the prepared batter among the coated muffin cups, filling each approximately 2/3 full with the prepared batter. Sprinkle with a bit of oats, followed by sugar. Bake in the preheated oven until a toothpick comes out clean, for 22 to 25 minutes.

Once done, place the muffin tin carefully on a cooling rack and let cool. Serve and enjoy.

Nutritional Value: kcal: 206, Fat: 7 g, Fiber: 3.2 g, Protein: 4.1 g

Galaxy Smoothie

Prep Time: 10 minutes

Cooking Time: 30 minutes

Servings: 4 persons

For a perfect edition, feel free to use honey as your sweetener & then troop them with the mini dark chocolate chips and frozen strawberries. You can even add an additional banana & mix in the cocoa powder and chopped almonds.

Ingredients

- 1 ripe banana
- ¼ cup maple syrup
- 1 organic egg, large-sized
- ½ cup almond milk
- 1 teaspoon vanilla extract
- 1 ½ cups rolled oats
- 1 teaspoon baking powder
- ½ cup Greek yogurt
- 1 teaspoon cinnamon
- Salt, as required, to taste

Optional Toppings:

- apple, sliced
- ½ cup dried cranberry
- blueberry
- strawberry, sliced
- nut, chopped (any of your favorite)
- dark chocolate chip

Directions

Preheat your oven to 350 F in advance.

Mash the banana in a large-sized mixing bowl until smooth, for a minute or two, and then, mix in the wet ingredients, give the ingredients a good stir and then, stir in the dry ingredients, continue to stir the ingredients until mixed thoroughly.

Lightly coat a standard-sized muffin tin (with 12 cups) and then, fill each cup approximately 2/3 full with the prepared batter.

Top each with the optional toppings.

Bake in the preheated oven until a toothpick comes out clean, for 30 minutes.

Serve and enjoy

Nutritional Value: kcal: 283, Fat: 3 g, Fiber: 4 g, Protein: 8 g

Mouthwatering Vanilla Muffins

Prep Time: 20 minutes

Cooking Time: 30 minutes

Servings: 12 persons

You can even use half and half of white sugar with cane sugar and it would still taste great. Serve chilled with almond milk and enjoy.

Ingredients

- ¼ cup melted butter, unsalted, cooled
- 1 ¼ cups flour
- ¼ teaspoon baking soda
- 1 teaspoon baking powder
- ½ cup granulated white sugar
- 1 organic egg, large-sized
- ¾ cup milk
- 1 teaspoon vanilla extract
- ¼ teaspoon salt

Directions

Add wheat flour with baking soda, baking powder and salt to a large-sized mixing bowl, whisk the ingredients until mixed well.

Add melted butter & sugar to a separate medium-sized mixing bowl.

Add egg to the wet mixture & beat until completely fluffy.

Add vanilla essence and milk to it, continue to beat the ingredients for a minute more.

Next, add this formed mixture into the flour mixture, whisk until mixed well, ensure that you don't over beat the ingredients.

Once done, line a muffin pan with muffin liners (preferably a double coating) and then, preheat your oven to 350 F in advance.

Fill each cup approximately ¾ full using an ice cream scooper & bake until a toothpick comes out clean, for 20 minutes.

Serve chilled and enjoy.

Nutritional Value: kcal: 88, Fat: 3.8 g, Fiber: 0.1 g, Protein: 1.3 g

Double Chocolate Muffins

Prep Time: 10 minutes

Cooking Time: 25 minutes

Servings: 12 persons

If you are looking for a vegan option, then you can replace the egg with unsweetened applesauce & use milk with lemon than the butter milk.

Ingredients

- 1 ½ cups all purpose flour
- 2 teaspoons baking powder
- ¾ cup Dutch cocoa powder
- 2 organic eggs, large-sized
- ½ teaspoon baking soda
- 2 teaspoons vanilla extract
- 1 cup granulated sugar
- 1 ¼ cup buttermilk
- ½ cup vegetable oil
- A heaping cup of chocolate chips
- ¾ teaspoon salt

Directions

Line a muffin tin (with 12 cups) with muffin liners and then, preheat your oven to 375 F in advance.

Whisk the flour with baking soda, cocoa powder, baking powder, and salt until mixed well. Once done, set the mixture aside.

Whisk the eggs with sugar, buttermilk, vanilla extract, and vegetable oil in a separate medium-sized mixing bowl.

Add the prepared flour mixture into the wet ingredients, continue to mix the ingredients until mixed well and then, fold in the chocolate chips.

Evenly divide the prepared batter among the muffin tins & bake in the preheated oven until a toothpick comes out clean, for 20 minutes.

Let the muffins to cool in the baking pan for a few minutes and then, completely cool on a baking rack. Serve and enjoy.

Nutritional Value: kcal: 222, Fat: 7.7 g, Fiber: 6 g, Protein: 4 g

Sugar-Crusted Raspberry Muffins

Prep Time: 20 minutes

Cooking Time: 30 minutes

Servings: 12 persons

You can use almond extract in place of vanilla and can use coconut sugar. Absolutely delicious & healthy!

Ingredients

- ½ cup melted unsalted butter
- 1 ½ cups raspberries, fresh
- ¼ teaspoon vanilla extract
- 2 cups all-purpose flour
- ¾ cup sugar
- 2 teaspoons baking powder
- ¾ cup whole milk
- 1 organic egg, large-sized
- ¼ teaspoon salt

Directions

Line a standard-sized muffin tin (12-cups) with paper liners or coat it with butter, cooking spray, or vegetable oil and then, preheat your oven to 400 F in advance.

Next, combine baking powder, 1 ¾ cups of flour with ½ cup sugar, and salt in a medium-sized mixing bowl until mixed well. Add in the butter & continue to mix the ingredients until combined well.

Whisk the milk with vanilla, and egg in a separate bowl. Slowly, add the milk mixture into the flour mixture, give the ingredients a good stir until just combined. Toss the berries with the leftover flour in a bowl and then, gently fold the prepared berry mixture into the prepared batter.

Fill each muffin cup approximately ¾ full and then, sprinkle the batter with the leftover sugar. Bake in the preheated oven until a toothpick comes out clean, for 17 to 20 minutes. Transfer the pan to a wire rack, set aside for 10 minutes to cool. Serve warm and enjoy.

Nutritional Value: kcal: 208, Fat: 7.4 g, Fiber: 1.4 g, Protein: 3.2 g

Cranberry Muffins

Prep Time: 10 minutes

Cooking Time: 40 minutes

Servings: 12 persons

Feel free to sub the dried cranberries with fresh ones. You can even use a loaf pan for this recipe.

Ingredients

- 1 cup dried cranberries
- 2 cups all purpose flour
- 1 cup softened unsalted butter, at room temperature
- 1 teaspoon orange zest
- 1 cup granulated sugar
- 1 teaspoon baking powder
- 2 organic eggs, large-sized
- ½ cup orange juice
- 1 teaspoon vanilla extract
- ½ teaspoon baking Soda

Directions

Line a standard-sized muffin tin with liners and then, preheat your oven to 350 F in advance.

Next, add butter with sugar in the bowl of your mixer, whisk until light & fluffy, for a couple of minutes.

Slowly add the eggs & continue to whisk the ingredients after each addition.

Add orange juice, vanilla extract and orange zest, continue to mix the ingredients until combined well.

Now add the cranberries, baking powder, baking soda and flour, continue to mix the ingredients until combined well.

Fill each muffin cup approximately ¾ full with the prepared batter.

Bake in the preheated oven until a toothpick comes out clean, for 25 to 30 minutes.

Remove the pan carefully from the hot oven & let cool for a couple of minutes. Serve warm and enjoy.

Nutritional Value: kcal: 317, Fat: 14 g, Fiber: 1 g, Protein: 2 g

Rhubarb Breakfast Muffins

Prep Time: 20 minutes

Cooking Time: 40 minutes

Servings: 12 persons

You would fall in love with the color and taste of this recipe. Feel free to add nuts of your choice to this recipe.

Ingredients

- ½ cup pure honey or maple syrup
- 1 large stalk rhubarb, trimmed & cut into ½" pieces
- ¼ cup all-purpose flour
- 1 teaspoon ground cinnamon
- ½ teaspoon baking powder
- 2 beaten eggs, large-sized
- ¼ cup extra-virgin coconut oil, melted
- 2 teaspoons pure vanilla extract
- ½ teaspoon kosher salt

Directions

Line a standard-size muffin pan (12 cups) with paper liners and then, preheat your oven to 375 F.

Next, whisk the flours with baking powder, cinnamon, and salt in a large-sized mixing bowl until mixed well.

Whisk the eggs with coconut oil, maple syrup, and vanilla in a medium-size mixing bowl. Fold the egg mixture gently into the flour mixture until just combined.

Evenly fill the muffin cups with the prepared batter & scatter 6 pieces of rhubarb on top of each muffin cup, pressing it partially into the batter.

Bake in the preheated oven for 22 to 25 minutes, until a wooden pick comes out clean. Let cool for 5 minutes in the pan and then, transfer to a wire rack to completely cool.

Nutritional Value: kcal: 229, Fat: 16 g, Fiber: 3 g, Protein: 6 g

Apricot-Oatmeal Muffins

Prep Time: 20 minutes

Cooking Time: 30 minutes

Servings: 6 persons

My grandmother used to prepare these delicious muffins for us. You can even add dried unsweetened mango as well. Feel free to sub the almond milk with cow milk.

Ingredients

- ¾ cup all-purpose flour
- ½ cup brown sugar, packed
- 1 tablespoon quick-cooking or old-fashioned oats
- ½ cup old-fashioned or quick-cooking oats
- 1 teaspoon baking powder
- 1/3 cup milk
- ½ teaspoon vanilla
- 1 organic egg, large-sized
- 1/3 cup dried apricots, finely chopped
- 3 tablespoons vegetable oil
- ¼ teaspoon salt

Directions

Grease the bottoms of 6 muffin cups (regular-sized) with cooking spray or shortening and then, preheat your oven to 400 F in advance.

Combine ½ cup oats with the flour, baking powder & salt in a medium-sized mixing bowl.

Next, combine the brown sugar with milk, egg, vanilla and oil using a wire whisk or fork in a small-sized mixing bowl until blended well.

Stir the milk mixture into the prepared flour mixture until the flour is just moistened and then, immediately fold in the apricots.

Evenly fill the muffin cups with the prepared batter and then, sprinkle each with approximately ½ teaspoon of oats.

Bake until a toothpick comes out clean, for 23 to 25 minutes. Remove from the pan to a cooling rack. Serve warm or cool.

Nutritional Value: kcal: 240, Fat: 8 g, Fiber: 1 g, Protein: 3 g

Eggless Mocha Muffins

Prep Time: 20 minutes

Cooking Time: 20 minutes

Servings: 12 persons

You can replace the unsweetened apple sauce with plain yogurt and can use any of your favorite nuts, such as hazelnuts or pecan in this recipe.

Ingredients

- 1 cup all purpose flour
- ⅓ cup canola oil or vegetable, corn or safflower
- 1 cup whole wheat flour
- ½ cup almonds, chopped
- 2 tablespoons cocoa powder, unsweetened
- ¼ teaspoon baking soda
- 2 ½ teaspoons baking powder
- ¼ cup unsweetened applesauce or plain yogurt
- 1 cup milk
- ½ cup white or dark chocolate chips
- 1 tablespoon Instant coffee
- ½ cup light brown sugar
- 1 teaspoon Pure vanilla extract
- ⅛ teaspoon salt

Directions

Line a muffin tray (with 12 cups) with muffin liners and then, preheat your oven to 400 F in advance.

Next, stir the coffee granules into the warm milk until completely dissolved. Warm up the milk in a microwave or on the stove top, ensure that you don't bring it to a boil.

Add in the instant coffee, give it a good stir & set aside.

In the meantime prepare the muffin batter.

Whisk both the flours with cocoa powder, baking powder, baking soda & salt in a large-sized mixing bowl until mixed well.

Sift the mixture well and set aside.

Now, whisk the brown sugar with oil in a large bowl. Whisk well.

Add in the applesauce & beat well.

Add in the dissolved coffee & continue to beat the ingredients.

Add the dry flour mixture and then, fold it in, ensure that you don't over beat the ingredients.

Add in your favorite nuts and the chocolate chips.

Fill the muffin tray evenly with the prepared batter.

Bake in the preheated oven for 18 to 20 minutes, until a toothpick comes out clean.

Remove & let the muffins to cool for 5 minutes into the pan then, remove to a cooling rack to completely cool. Serve and enjoy.

Nutritional Value: kcal: 194, Fat: 11 g, Fiber: 1.2 g, Protein: 3.4 g

Cinnamon Sugar Pumpkin Muffins

Prep Time: 20 minutes

Cooking Time: 30 minutes

Servings: 12 persons

These pumpkin muffins are easy to prepare and are super moist. For ultimate breakfast, just top them with the sugar-cinnamon mixture and enjoy.

Ingredients

For Pumpkin Muffins:

- 1 ½ cups pumpkin puree, canned
- 2 cups all-purpose flour
- ½ teaspoon baking soda
- 2 organic eggs, large-sized
- 1 tablespoon ground cinnamon
- 1 teaspoon baking powder
- 1 ½ teaspoons ground nutmeg
- ½ cup brown sugar, packed
- 1 cup granulated sugar
- ¼ cup milk
- ½ cup unsalted melted butter
- 1 teaspoon ground ginger
- 2 teaspoons vanilla extract
- ½ teaspoon salt
- ½ teaspoon ground cloves

For Sugar Cinnamon Coating:

- 4 teaspoon ground cinnamon
- 3 tablespoons melted unsalted butter
- ¼ cup sugar

Directions

Line a standard-sized muffin pan with liners and then, preheat your oven to 350 F in advance.

Combine the flour with spices, baking soda, baking powder and salt in a medium sized mixing bowl until mixed well, set the mixture aside.

Next, combine the melted butter with sugars in a large-sized mixing bowl, whisk the ingredients until combined well.

Add the milk & whisk until combined well.

Add in the eggs, vanilla extract and pumpkin puree, whisk until combined well.

Add the mixture of dry ingredients into the mixture of wet ingredients, whisk until just combined, ensure that you don't over mix the ingredients.

Fill the prepared muffins liners approximately ¾ full with the prepared batter.

Bake until a toothpick comes out clean, for 18 to 24 minutes.

Remove the muffins carefully from the hot oven & let cool.

Combine the ground cinnamon and sugar in a small-sized mixing bowl until mixed well.

Brush the tops of muffins with the melted butter and then, turn the muffin & coat each with the sugar-cinnamon mixture.

Store muffins at room temperature in an airtight container.

Nutritional Value: kcal: 262, Fat: 10 g, Fiber: 4 g, Protein: 3.2 g

Potato Crust Chicken Muffins

Prep Time: 2 minutes

Cooking Time: 2 minutes

Servings: 1 person

Garnish your muffins with fresh rosemary and enjoy. You can even enjoy these muffins as a lunch recipe. Just serve these muffins with freshly prepared mint chutney and enjoy the taste.

Ingredients

- 3 potatoes
- ½ red bell pepper
- 1 onion
- ½ cup mozzarella, shredded
- 10 ounces of chicken breast
- ½ yellow bell pepper
- 2 carrots, shredded

Directions

Fill a pot with water and bring it to a boil, over moderate heat. Once done, add the chicken, cover with a lid & cook for 12 to 15 minutes.

Preheat your oven to 360 F in advance.

Chop the onion and bell peppers then, slice the chicken.

Next, over moderate heat in a large skillet, heat up the vegetable oil & add the veggies. Cook for 2 to 3 minutes.

Thinly slice the potatoes.

Cover the empty holes of a muffin tray and with potato slices, adding the slices on sides as well.

Fill with the cooked chicken, veggies, and mozzarella.

Bake in the preheated oven for 20 to 25 minutes, serve warm and enjoy.

Nutritional Value: kcal: 240, Fat: 8 g, Fiber: 4 g, Protein: 16 g

Delicious Meatloaf Muffins

Prep Time: 10 minutes

Cooking Time: 20 minutes

Servings: 11 persons

You can even use coconut amnions and bread crumbs in this recipe. For added nutrition, feel free to add a bit of full-fat mozzarella cheese into each muffin cup.

Ingredients

- 1 pound ground beef
- ¼ teaspoon garlic powder
- 1 cup onion, chopped
- ¼ teaspoon onion powder
- 1 organic egg, large-sized
- ¼ teaspoon black pepper
- 1 cup pork panko
- ¼ teaspoon Italian seasoning
- 5 ½ tablespoons unsweetened ketchup
- ¼ teaspoon salt

Directions

Coat a muffin pan lightly with butter and then, preheat your oven to 350 F in advance.

Next, combine the ground beef with chopped onion, garlic powder, pork panko, egg, Italian seasoning, onion powder, pepper and salt in a large-sized mixing bowl, knead until combined well.

Fill the muffin pan with approximately ¼ cup of the prepared mixture (you should be having approximately 11 muffins)

Top each cup with ½ tablespoon of Ketchup and bake in the preheated oven for 12 to 15 minutes.

Nutritional Value: kcal: 161, Fat: 10 g, Fiber: 3.1 g, Protein: 14.2 g

Date Muffins

Prep Time: 25 minutes

Cooking Time: 20 minutes

Servings: 8 persons

The best part about these muffins is that you can freeze them for up to 3 months. Just before eating, simply warm the muffins a bit in a microwave.

Ingredients

- ½ cup dates, chopped
- 1 organic egg, large-sized
- ½ teaspoon baking powder
- ¼ cup shortening
- ½ cup sugar
- 1 cup all-purpose flour
- ¼ teaspoon ground cinnamon
- ½ teaspoon baking soda
- ¼ cup walnuts, chopped
- ½ cup boiling water

Directions

Fill a small bowl with the boiling water and then, add the dates, let stand for a couple of minutes (don't drain). In the meantime, beat the shortening with sugar in a small-sized mixing bowl for a minute or two, until crumbly and then, beat in the egg.

Add dates & continue to beat the ingredient until blended, on low speed. Once done, combine the flour with baking soda, baking powder & cinnamon then, immediately stir into prepared date mixture using a large wooden spoon until just blended. Once done, stir in the walnuts.

Pour the mixture evenly into paper-lined muffin cups, filling each cup approximately 2/3 full.

Bake until a toothpick comes out clean, for 15 to 20 minutes, at 350 F. Let cool for a couple of minutes then, remove from pan to a wire rack to completely cool.

Nutritional Value: kcal: 212, Fat: 8 g, Fiber: 1 g, Protein: 3 g

Date Carrot Muffins

Prep Time: 10 minutes

Cooking Time: 20 minutes

Servings: 12 persons

You can pack these muffins and can eat them as lunch too. You can use regular oats and can use cashew milk too.

Ingredients

- 1 cup steel cut quick oats
- ½ cup brown sugar
- 1 teaspoon baking powder
- ½ teaspoon baking soda
- 1 cup flour
- 2 teaspoons ground cinnamon
- 1 cup carrot, finely shredded
- ½ cup dates, roughly chopped
- 1 large egg beaten
- 2 teaspoons vanilla extract
- ¼ cup vegetable oil
- 1 cup milk
- ½ teaspoon salt

Directions

Combine all of the dry ingredients together in a large-sized mixing bowl until mixed well.

Add dates, gently toss the ingredients until coated well. Feel free to break up any clumps of date.

Add the shredded carrot, toss again to coat and ensure that there are no clumps remain.

Beat the egg with oil, vanilla and milk in a small-sized mixing bowl.

Pour into the prepared flour mixture, give the ingredients a good stir until combined well.

Fill paper lined muffins tins with the prepared batter (approximately ¾ full).

Bake for 20 to 25 minutes, until a toothpick comes out clean, at 400 F. Enjoy.

Nutritional Value: kcal: 214, Fat: 6.2 g, Fiber: 3.1 g, Protein: 4.2 g

Whole Wheat Apple Cinnamon Muffins

Prep Time: 20 minutes

Cooking Time: 25 minutes

Servings: 15 persons

Feel free to sub the oil with melted coconut oil. My kids just love to have these muffins as breakfast! Smell and tastes delicious!

Ingredients

- 1 teaspoon baking soda
- 2 cups whole wheat flour
- ½ teaspoon allspice
- 1 teaspoon baking powder
- 1/3 cup unsweetened applesauce
- 2 teaspoons ground cinnamon
- ½ cup pecans, chopped
- 3 organic eggs, large-sized
- 2/3 cup pure maple syrup
- 2 cups apple, grated/shredded
- 1/3 cup canola or vegetable oil
- 1 ½ teaspoons pure vanilla extract
- ½ teaspoon salt

Directions

Coat a muffin pan (12-cups) with nonstick spray or line them with cupcake liners (repeat for the leftover three muffins) and then, preheat your oven to 425 F.

Whisk the flour with cinnamon, baking powder, baking soda, allspice, pecans, and salt in a large-sized mixing bowl until combined well, set the mixture aside. Next, whisk the eggs with oil, maple syrup, vanilla, and applesauce in a medium-sized mixing bowl until combined well. Pour the mixture of wet ingredients into the mixture of dry ingredients, give it a good stir and then, add in the grated/shredded apple. Gently fold the ingredients until no flour pockets remain & just combined.

Fill the prepared muffin cups with approximately ¾ full with the prepared batter and then, bake at 425 F for 5 minutes then decrease the oven temperature to 350 F & bake for 18 more minutes, until a toothpick comes out clean. Let cool in the muffin pan for a couple of minutes and then, transfer to a wire rack to completely cool.

Nutritional Value: kcal: 240, Fat: 8 g, Fiber: 3.2 g, Protein: 4 g

Red Currant Muffins

Prep Time: 10 minutes

Cooking Time: 30 minutes

Servings: 12 persons

Silver almonds and coarse sugar are optional; however, these two ingredients increase the taste of muffins. I generally served mine with a glass full of milk and my family just loves it.

Ingredients

- 1 cup sugar
- 2 cups red currants
- 1 ½ cups all-purpose flour
- ½ cup whole wheat flour
- 1 tablespoon baking powder
- ½ cup milk
- 1 ½ teaspoons vanilla extract
- ½ cup butter, melted
- 2 organic eggs, large-sized
- ½ teaspoon salt

Optional Ingredients:

- Coarse sugar for sprinkling
- ¼ cup slivered almonds

Directions

Line muffin tins with the liners and then, preheat your oven to 375 F in advance.

Next, whisk the flours with baking powder, sugar and salt in a medium to large-sized mixing bowl until mixed well, set the mixture aside.

Whisk the milk with melted butter, extract and eggs in a small-sized liquid measuring cup or bowl. Pour this mixture on top of the dry ingredients & continue to mix the ingredients until just combined. Fold in the currants, keep ½ cup of currants aside to top.

Fill each muffin cups approximately ¾ full with the prepared batter & garnish each cup with the kept-aside currants & sugar or almonds. Ensure that you don't over-fill the cups. Bake in the preheated oven until turn golden brown & a toothpick comes out clean, for 25 to 30 minutes.

Nutritional Value: kcal: 284, Fat: 7.6 g, Fiber: 7.2 g, Protein: 11 g

Orange-Currant Muffins

Prep Time: 20 minutes

Cooking Time: 40 minutes

Servings: 12 persons

A nice way to kick-start your day! I often serve these muffins with freshly squeezed orange juice and a few orange slices. Absolutely delicious and healthy!

Ingredients

- 2 ¼ cups all-purpose flour
- ¼ cup orange juice concentrate, frozen & thawed
- 2 teaspoons orange peel, grated
- ¾ cup milk
- 1 slightly beaten egg, large-sized
- ½ cup sugar
- 3 teaspoons baking powder
- ¼ cup raisins or currants
- 1 teaspoon orange peel, grated
- 1/3 cup vegetable oil
- 3 tablespoons sugar
- ¼ teaspoon salt

Directions

Line a standard sized muffin tin with muffin liners and then, preheat your oven to 400 F.

Beat the milk with juice concentrate, oil, the egg & 2 teaspoons orange peel in a large-sized mixing bowl until blended well. Once done, stir in the flour followed by ½ cup of sugar, baking powder & salt until the flour is just moistened then, fold in the currants or raisins.

Evenly divide the prepared batter among the muffin cups. Mix 1 teaspoon orange peel and 3 tablespoons of sugar then, sprinkle on top of the batter in the cups.

Bake until turn light golden brown, for 20 to 25 minutes. Immediately remove from the pan. Serve immediately and enjoy.

Nutritional Value: kcal: 214, Fat: 4.2 g, Fiber: 1.3 g, Protein: 3.0 g

Bran Muffins

Prep Time: 20 minutes

Cooking Time: 35 minutes

Servings: 12 persons

Enjoy these delicious muffins on your breakfast table. Feel free to add ½ cup of raisins and 1 cup of chopped dates to your muffins.

Ingredients

- 2 cups bran cereal flakes or 1 ¼ cups cereal
- ½ teaspoon vanilla
- 1 ¼ cups all-purpose flour
- ½ cup brown sugar, packed
- 3 teaspoons baking powder
- 1 organic egg, large-sized
- ¼ teaspoon ground cinnamon
- ¼ cup vegetable oil
- 1 1/3 cups milk
- ¼ teaspoon salt

Directions

Fill each of muffin cups with a paper baking cup and then, preheat your oven to 400 F in advance.

Next roll the cereal in a large re-sealable plastic bag using a rolling pin & crush the cereal into fine crumbs.

Stir the crushed cereal with milk, vanilla and raisins in a medium-sized mixing bowl until mixed well. Let stand until cereal has softened, for a couple of minutes. Beat in the egg and oil using a fork.

Stir the flour with baking powder, brown sugar, cinnamon and salt in a separate medium-sized mixing bowl until mixed well. Stir the prepared flour mixture into the cereal mixture until the flour is just moistened. Evenly divide the prepared cups with the batter.

Bake until a toothpick comes out clean, for 20 to 25 minutes. Once done, let cool in the pan for 5 minutes, remove to a cooling rack and let completely cool. Serve immediately and enjoy.

Nutritional Value: kcal: 216, Fat: 7 g, Fiber: 4 g, Protein: 6.1 g

Apple-Cream Cheese Muffins

Prep Time: 30 minutes

Cooking Time: 40 minutes

Servings: 15 persons

One of the best muffins I have ever prepared. Whenever I prepare these muffins, it gets disappeared within a few minutes.

Ingredients

For Streusel

- 3 tablespoons brown sugar, packed
- 1 tablespoon margarine or butter, softened
- 2 tablespoons all-purpose flour

For Muffins

- 1/3 cup cream cheese
- 1 apple, large, peeled & shredded
- ¾ cup brown sugar, packed
- ½ teaspoon salt
- 1 ¾ cups all-purpose flour
- ¼ cup applesauce
- 1 teaspoon baking powder
- ½ teaspoon ground cinnamon
- 2 beaten eggs, large-sized
- 2/3 cup oil
- 1 teaspoon vanilla

Directions

Line 15 muffin cups with paper baking cups and then, preheat your oven to 350 F in advance. Reserve approximately 1 tablespoon of brown sugar in muffins for filling.

Next, combine the leftover brown sugar with 1 ¾ cups flour, baking powder, cinnamon and salt using an electric mixer in a large bowl until mixed well, on low speed. Reserve 1 tablespoon of beaten egg for filling. Add applesauce, oil, leftover egg and vanilla to the flour mixture. Continue to beat the ingredients until mixed well, on medium speed. Once done, stir in the apple using a spoon.

Now, combine the cream cheese with the kept-aside brown sugar & reserved egg in a small-sized mixing bowl. Fill each muffin cups approximately 2/3 full with the prepared batter. Top each with 1 teaspoon of the cream cheese mixture and then, top with spoonful of the leftover batter. Combine all of the streusel ingredients together in a small-sized mixing bowl, sprinkle on top of the batter.

Bake in the preheated oven until a toothpick comes out clean, for 22 to 26 minutes. Remove from the pan & let slightly cool for 8 to 10 minutes.

Nutritional Value: kcal: 230, Fat: 11 g, Fiber: 1 g, Protein: 3 g

Carrot Currant Muffins

Prep Time: 20 minutes

Cooking Time: 20 minutes

Servings: 12 persons

Feel free to top your muffins with a sugar-cinnamon mixture. You can even garnish your muffins with homemade icing and chopped nuts.

Ingredients

- 1/3 cup packed brown sugar
- ¼ cup plain Greek yogurt
- 1 cup old-fashioned rolled oats
- ½ teaspoon baking soda
- 1 tablespoon vinegar
- ¼ teaspoon allspice
- 1 cup all-purpose flour
- ¼ cup whole wheat flour or white whole wheat flour
- 1 teaspoon baking powder
- ¾ cup dairy-free milk or normal milk
- 1 teaspoon ground cinnamon
- 1/8 teaspoon ground nutmeg
- ¼ cup unsweetened applesauce
- 1 organic egg, large
- ¼ teaspoon vanilla
- 1/3 cup currants
- 1 cup carrots, shredded or grated
- ½ cup baking walnuts, chopped
- ¼ cup butter, melted & slightly cooled
- ¼ teaspoon salt

Directions

Combine oats with milk, yogurt and vinegar in a large-sized mixing bowl, give the ingredients a good stir & let sit until the oats soften, for an hour.

Next, lightly coat a non-stick muffin pan with butter and then, preheat your oven to 375 F in advance.

Combine flours with allspice, baking powder, nutmeg, baking soda, cinnamon, and salt in a separate medium-sized mixing bowl.

Stir egg with vanilla, applesauce, brown sugar, butter, currants, and carrots in the bowl with oat mixture, continue to mix the ingredients using a fork until incorporated well.

Whisk the dry ingredients together and slowly sift the prepared flour mixture into the carrot mixture using a sieve or a sifter. Once done, give the ingredients a good stir using a fork until just combined.

Once done, immediately fold in the walnuts.

Fill the prepared muffin tin approximately ¾ full with the prepared batter.

Bake in the preheated oven until a toothpick comes out clean, for 15 to 20 minutes. Set aside on a wire rack to completely cool. Serve and enjoy.

Nutritional Value: kcal: 185, Fat: 8 g, Fiber: 2 g, Protein: 4.6 g

Mini Blueberry Muffins with Streusel

Prep Time: 20 minutes

Cooking Time: 30 minutes

Servings: 12 persons

We all enjoyed this wonderful gluten-free muffin recipe on the breakfast table. You can sub the almond milk with any of your favorite milk and enjoy.

Ingredients

For Muffins:

- ¾ teaspoon xanthan gum
- 1 cup blueberries, fresh
- ¾ teaspoon baking soda
- ½ cup sugar
- 1 ½ cups all-purpose rice flour blend, gluten free
- ½ teaspoon gluten-free baking powder
- 2 organic eggs, large
- ¼ cup melted coconut oil
- ½ teaspoon ground cinnamon
- 1 cup almond milk
- ¼ teaspoon salt

For Streusel:

- 2 tablespoons all-purpose rice flour blend, gluten free
- ¼ cup oats, gluten-free
- 1 teaspoon water
- ¼ cup walnuts, chopped
- 1 tablespoon coconut oil
- 1/3 cup light brown sugar

Directions

Coat 24 mini muffin cups lightly with the cooking spray and then, preheat your oven to 350 F in advance.

Next, combine all of the streusel ingredients together in a medium-sized mixing bowl until mixed well, set the mixture aside.

Combine 1 ½ cups flour blend with baking powder, xanthan gum, baking soda, cinnamon & salt in a large-sized mixing bowl, beating well using a whisk. Add the leftover ingredients & lastly fold in the fresh blueberries. Evenly fill the muffin cups with the prepared batter. Top each cup with a teaspoon of the streusel.

Bake in the preheated oven until a toothpick comes out clean, for 20 to 25 minutes. Transfer to a wire rack and let cool for 10 minutes, serve and enjoy.

Nutritional Value: kcal: 204, Fat: 8 g, Fiber: 1 g, Protein: 2 g

Conclusion

Thank you again for choosing this book.

With this book, you can get plenty of options to prepare muffin recipes. Muffins are famous worldwide and these recipes don't need any special ingredient.

You can surprise your kiddos and your family just by preparing their favorite muffin recipe for breakfast.

With these muffin recipes, your body would naturally get essential vitamins and minerals. Your body would get enough of antioxidants through fresh raw vegetables and fruits.

What are you still waiting for? If you haven't bought this book yet, then do it now, turn the pages, and surprise your family with your smoothie-making techniques.

About the Author

Born in New Germantown, Pennsylvania, Stephanie Sharp received a Masters degree from Penn State in English Literature. Driven by her passion to create culinary masterpieces, she applied and was accepted to The International Culinary School of the Art Institute where she excelled in French cuisine. She has married her cooking skills with an aptitude for business by opening her own small cooking school where she teaches students of all ages.

Stephanie's talents extend to being an author as well and she has written over 400 e-books on the art of cooking and baking that include her most popular recipes.

Sharp has been fortunate enough to raise a family near her hometown in Pennsylvania where she, her husband and children live in a beautiful rustic house on an extensive piece of land. Her other passion is taking care of the furry members of her family which include 3 cats, 2 dogs and a potbelly pig named Wilbur.

Watch for more amazing books by Stephanie Sharp coming out in the next few months.

Author's Afterthoughts

I am truly grateful to you for taking the time to read my book. I cherish all of my readers! Thanks ever so much to each of my cherished readers for investing the time to read this book!

With so many options available to you, your choice to buy my book is an honour, so my heartfelt thanks at reading it from beginning to end!

I value your feedback, so please take a moment to submit an honest and open review on Amazon so I can get valuable insight into my readers' opinions and others can benefit from your experience.

Thank you for taking the time to review!

Stephanie Sharp

For announcements about new releases, please follow my author page on Amazon.com!

You can find that at:

https://www.amazon.com/author/stephanie-sharp

*or Scan **QR-code** below.*